MORE POEMS ABOUT PURPLE WIZARDS AND NEON BRICKT EXCEPTIONALISMS

More Poems about Purple Wizards
and
Neon-Bright Exceptionalisms

Jason Preu

EMP Books
Kansas City, MO
www.EMPbooks.com

Copyright © 2017 by Jason Preu

All rights reserved. No part of this book may be reproduced, scanned, or distributed in any printed or electronic form, including information storage and retrieval systems, without permission. Please do not participate in or encourage piracy of copyrighted materials in violation of the author's rights. Please purchase only authorized editions.

First Edition: 11 7 5 3 2 1
ISBN: 978-0-9985077-6-7
Library of Congress Control Number: 2017947681

This book is a work of fiction. Names, characters, places, dates, scientific theories, memories from your childhood, and incidents are products of the author's imagination, or are used fictitiously, satirically, or as parody or shaktipat. Any resemblance to actual persons, living, dead, or undead, business establishments, events, or locales is entirely coincidental, unless you are a purple wizard. In that case, everything is on purpose.

Design, Layout, and Edits: Jeanette Powers
Cover & Interior Art: Sarah, Roman, and Beatrix Preu
title font: Undercover by Jakob Fischer at pizzadude.dk

Doug, this is for you.
Everywhere now you are now everything.

Part 1 – Arrival/Hate/Culture/Worry

What They Say About That Dude
Pro Soccer
Metastoicheiosis
Draw Me like One of Your French Girls
Top Guns
Open Up and Say Agar.Io
Iron Maidens
War Operation Plan Response
Some Things Are and Some Things Aren't
The Diagnostic Artifact Recognizes Itself and Decides Nietzsche Was Onto Something
Social Anxieties That Will Not Be Cured By SSRIs Alone
BYOB
We Carry All Of The Power We Need Inside Ourselves Already
~~Playing Excitebike with LL Cool J~~

Part 2 – Entrenchment/Love/Others/Confusion

What We Mean When We Don't Say What We Mean
Three Sentences about You, Us, and Me
I Ought To Understand Frailty
Breaking the Cycle of Refrigeration
Red Light Green Light
Country Lament #252
Florimell's Parallel
Life Longs For Itself
A Rhetorical Question Is A Figure Of Speech In The Form Of A Question That Is Asked In Order To Make A Point Rather Than To Elicit An Answer
The Androgen Paradox

Part 3 – Departure/Change/Self/Loss

Prayer of the Magi
Things Played out Much Differently in Earlier Versions of How We'd End Up
The Ice Cream Man Is Coming
I Seem To Recall Being Shown A Way
You Can't Fix Everything Forever
Like Light, This Expands and We Never Get Where We're Going
Ornithology Abandons Athena
Next Time You're Feeling Blue Just Let a Smile Begin, Happy Things Will Come To You
The Afterparty
Never Trust a Heavenly Body
Future Deaths Leave A Stained Past From Whence Are Born Children of Night
Muttering To Oneself, Curious
Us V. Them
Hemimetaboly Makes the Heart Grow Fonder
As Falls
The Silence over Oppression by Otherwise Good People
Once Broken, Then Open
The Older One Recognizes, Regrets, and Attempts to Rectify the Situation
We Fear We Have Frighted
Royal and Wrinkled With Age

Appendix Q – Spontaneous Combustion/Enlightenment

PART 1
ARRIVAL/HATE/CULTURE/WORRY

The Purple Wizard exits from a dark forest green.

The Purple Wizard is out of time, is not of time.

The Purple Wizard lives again to tell
                      of hate, of love, of change.

The Purple Wizard sings eternally
                      for the Purple Wizard knows
                      we are the hard of hearing.

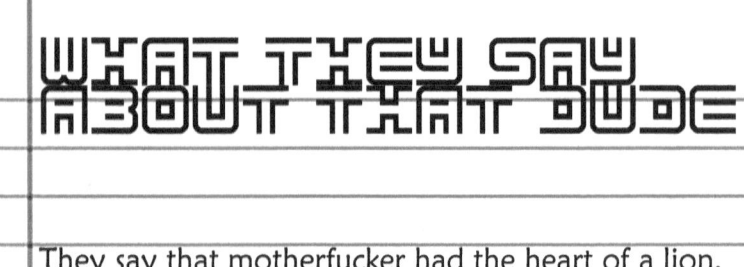

WHAT THEY SAY ABOUT THAT DUDE

They say that motherfucker had the heart of a lion,
   a dragon,
      a Chihuahua,
         a butterfly,
   an earthworm,
  the heart of Balls-Out-Billings, Montana.
But that dude's heart's just beat, man.

And its beats, man?
Those rhythms are most unkind.

PRO SOCCER

Once came a youthful hero
who could kick a ball
straight through a brick wall.

Drafted then, paid to deliver
that ball through other people –
their bellies, their heads.

Ruddy god among ball kickers
divine piston legs
indifferent to defenses.

Ball blockers, ball stoppers world-wide
soon refused to play for they
wished not for chests with gaping holes.

Still, they were paid handsomely
to stand hard and die holey.
Sport often makes no sense.

METASTOICHEIOSIS

Father stands before them, says
"The bread is life eternal."
Two six-year-old girls
sit close, listening, watching.
>One has twisted a tissue
>into a pointed pick
>which she thrusts repeatedly
>into her right nostril.

She thrusts, then inspects,
then thrusts, then inspects,
until, at long last,
her efforts are rewarded.
>She smiles a toothy, wide relief
>and shows the fruits of her labor
>to her silent, attentive neighbor
>who nods a curt approval.

"There is life eternal," Father says,
"And that is the good news."
"In fact," he continues, arms raising,
"What news in this world could be better?"

DRAW ME LIKE ONE OF YOUR FRENCH GIRLS *

                      until the iceberg comes,
            we'll spin tales about suicidal propellers
             and we'll lie naked for the lower classes
     and we'll make it count between cold crests.

                      until the iceberg comes,
              we'll taunt them rich sunsabitches
          and we'll dress like them, steal their jackets
  and we'll drag their women through the icy blues.

                      until the iceberg comes,
             we'll make new love in Model T Fords
     and we'll spin sick under electric orange lights
and we'll run like pale rats through an iron-walled maze.

but when that iceberg comes, oh when that frozen chunk of humility comes, that tiny speck in an otherwise infinite ocean of circumstance comes, it comes hard, rips us a new one or two, fills our empty holes with a few precious hours of unexpected, impossible meaning, it comes when it comes so silent so deep in the dark, oh! when that iceberg comes, how it comes! how it comes! how it comes!

                      *Translated from the original Anglo-Saxon folk tale

TOP GUMS

I am Goose

And I am Hollywood

And I am Maverick

And I am Viper

And I am Jester

And I am Cougar

And I am Slider

And I am Stinger

And I am Sundown

And I am Chipper

And I am Ghostrider

And I am Voodoo 3

And I am Mustang

And I am Blade

And I am TEX

And I am Rat

And I am Heater

And I am Iceman

And I am Merlin

And I am Wolfman

And I am Charlie, too

And I am sand volleyball
Losing my loving feelings
Whilst flying a Grumman F-14
Tomcat in an inverted vertical
Flipping birds to some Ruskies
Flying make-believe MiG-28s
Goddamn!
I am the killer of Russians
Goddammit!
Goddamn! Yes, they had it coming
Watching every motion in their neverwere MiGs

I AM a tone engaged flyby losing you forever
For I AM forever heading into twilight
And I AM taking breaths away with the boys
In the goddamn danger zone
And yes! Goddamn! Goddammit, yes!
I AM the mirror crashing
And I AM
every
single
simple
goddamn
joy
!

OPEN UP AND SAY AGAR.IO

Be eaten or eat and grow and watch out and move fast and consume and consume and grow bigger and be eaten or eat and hide and hide and move fast to skirt-kite-escape biggers and be eaten or eat and grow big and touch a virus – blow into a million and one little bits of all you split – infected – and float and run and hide and be vulnerable be eaten and start again and name yourself something good and different and meaningless and mean and new and different and new and over again and be eaten or eat and stalk smallers now so many others – smallers hoping to get biggers - to have their name grace a leader-board for two-five-ten minutes get gargantuan thirty-five minutes like life like politics like life move like love move like life move like us move like God move you and me to press Play to be eaten or eat to grow big and bigger to grow and eat and eat to run and hide and move fast to die and start over again.

IRON MAIDENS

The number of **The Beast is** U.S.: (555)-401-2233.

You may call The Beast for a **good** time.
You may **call The Beast** when you're feeling blue.

You may call The Beast any, anytime.
You may **call The Beast**, maybe.

You may call The Beast Betty
and when The Beast calls you
The Beast will call you Al.

You may call **The Beast** in the morning
after you've taken two of these.
If **you** get **The Beast**'s voicemail
do leave a message.

The Beast will call you back
at The Beast's earliest convenience.

WAR OPERATION PLAN RESPONSE

We all knew what would happen
    when you pressed that button.
So red and juicy, so full of warning,
    begging for your trigger finger's touch.
We all knew it felt so damned good. Didn't it?
Did you press it slow and steady, savoring the end?
Or did you do it quickly, no time
    for remorse or second guesses?
Did you check your phone
    one last time for any messages?
Did you whisper goodbye to anything or anyone?
Did you pause to wonder what kind of creatures
    might rest the fate of their existence on a fat red button?
Did you find you couldn't say no?
    Couldn't refuse? Couldn't turn around and walk away?
Who were you helping?
What color your eyes! Grey-blue in a bright room!
Do you remember how we met?
Do you remember my blouse
    with the one missing button?
Do you want to play a game?

SOME THINGS ARE AND SOME THINGS ARE NOT

Don't you dare call this a poem. Whatever it may be: cry for help, sheer desperation, attention-whoring, click-baiting, self-indulgence– it ain't no poem. It ain't no poem 'cause a poem's got 🪶 and legs and 👣 and movement and breadth and 💡 – a poem is a goddamn 🎩 – and this is an unholy, molten 🌋, red red 👹 from way underground. So don't call it a poem. Especially since it's about you and you know you ain't down to be associated with poetry. Who really is down for that these days? Down to march through mired meter getting hands and knees all soiled trying to separate out crust-covered mixed metaphors which get you digging further and further till you're so deep down you're dripping sweat from the earth's burning core? Naw, this ain't no poem. This ain't no metaphor. It's about you. This ain't no 🎵. This is just some words looking for an open 👀 or 👂 and a nutritious 🧠 to get down into, to take root, to propagate, to infiltrate, to overgrow and drag ya down deep like some 👹 weed.

THE DIAGNOSTIC ARTIFACT RECOGNIZES ITSELF AND DECIDES NIETZSCHE WAS ONTO SOMETHING

While scratching an itch in a budget meeting I find under my skin something glowing like a bright bronze idol. Being a prospector of some repute, I excuse myself to the 8th floor restroom. Cinnafresh air welcomes me and the far stall waits unoccupied. Starting at my fingernail, I carefully peel my skin away; thin, pale strip after thin, pale strip, which I pile into the corner behind the toilet. It takes some time and when I've finished with my left arm, I pause to examine my limb under the white fluorescents – something of value there, long-hidden indeed.

I continue in this manner for hours and hours
   listening
      to the clickclackclick

                    of hard plastic shoe heels
                    and the zooooop
                        of slippery zippers
                                    and flush
                            after flush
                    after flush.

                                            I peel.
                                            I pile.
        Until the 5 o'clock bell sounds, I peel and pile.

My co-workers rush home and the halls echo an eerie absent nothing. My skin is a mound of strips piled higher than the toilet seat. Is it still me sitting there in the quiet hours after work, my body something else and my face surely peeled away? I wrangle open the lock, slowed by the texture of my own hands, and I walk on aged bronzed tiptoes to a mirror placed above three sinks. I cannot stare for long, those eyes watching from unknown sockets, thin, ornamental fingertips tracing my new, ancient jawline. The halls reverberate my heavy steps. I leave my work bags in my cubicle and take the elevator down to the lobby. You should have seen the look on the security guards' faces as I walked out those revolving doors.

SOCIAL ANXIETIES THAT WILL NOT BE CURED BY SSRIS ALONE

There are 5,323,208,384
unread messages
in your in-box ...
one is from him.

You made me a playlist.
I wanted a mixtape.

She always retweets.
You always favorite.

Facebook was your happy place
before all your real friends showed up.

If Instagram had shown him anything,
it's that he loved only fine foods
and island vacations

and yoga pants.

They watched
you disappear
in Snapchat.

For days
they cried
real tears.

34�03

Open the cooler
                the cooler
Dump in the ice
                the ice
Crawl into the cooler
                the cooler
Bury yourself in the ice
                the ice
Close the cooler
                the cooler
Subsist on the ice
                the ice
Wait inside the cooler
                the cooler
Wait deep down in the ice
                the ice

And when that cooler lid cracks open, wake yourself and watch for a warm hand blindly reaching for an icy bottle; offer your frozen grip instead and clasp tight, give a firm shake. Let that unseen seeker know you're a man, a cold and collapsible man, very refreshing and able to offer a real insider's perspective on what it takes to be thermally dynamic.

WE CARRY ALL OF THE POWER WE NEED INSIDE OURSELVES ALREADY

I am looking at you   this way
    because I am trying to melt your face with my mind,
      trying to destroy you in a most peculiar way –
a most painful and peculiar and wholly unforgettable way
        so don't you turn from me just yet.

Keep your eyes opened, focused.

I want you to watch as they drop from your head,
   your eyes, want to watch you watching yourself
disintegrate, want to watch you watching yourself pool
into a gooey mess, want you to write me a song about
    yourself as a gooey mess on the kitchen floor
write me a murder ballad with piano and upright bass,
a ballad about how I melted your face with my mind –
               my mind:
              pure hate,
           willful annihilation.

PART 2
ENTRENCHMENT/LOVE/OTHERS/CONFUSION

The Purple Wizard is right on time,
                is not a machine of productivity.

The Purple Wizard screams among us
                always and we love to look aside.

The Purple Wizard exists within red hearts blue.

The Purple Wizard loves to sell charms
                of spun gold dreams.

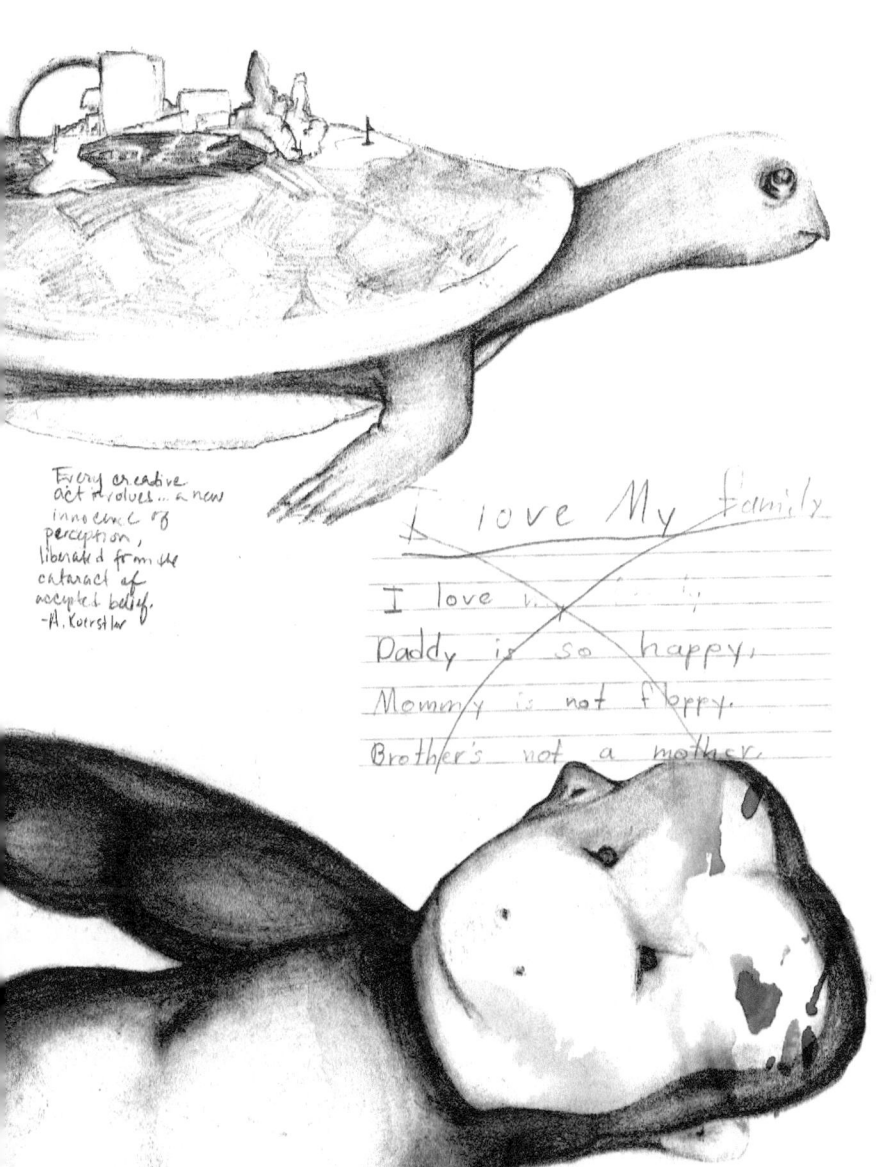

Every creative act involves... a new innocence of perception, liberated from the cataract of accepted belief.
-A. Koestler

I love My family
I love ~~...~~
Daddy is so happy.
Mommy is not floppy.
Brother's not a mother.

What We Mean When We Do Not Say What We Mean

When you whisper in my ear
    it's like a million miniature feathers
    tickling my skin, and I pause
    to wonder if, somewhere
    deep down in your lungs,
    a million tiny birds live
    fluttering, song-filled lives.

And, if so, are their songs also your songs?

Are their laments and losses and loves
    also yours to croon about?

And do your throat and mouth ever grow dry?

THREE SENTENCES ABOUT YOU US AND ME

You juggle slippery ellipses,
unaware of your shadow's impact
upon the seasoned growth underfoot.

We sit,
cross-legged
between uncanny stars,
contemplating our lack of development,
this stunted growth,
and how restrictive the speed of light.

The grammar of ploughed fields
circumscribes me
and in twilight I sip
the lightning bugs' glow.

I OUGHT TO UNDERSTAND FRAILTY

Across a stained, wooden table
    our daughter reads a comic book
    about a babysitter with diabetes.

We wait for hot chocolate
    at a packed coffee shop
    a short drive from our house.

This is a description of that moment.

Our daughter's chin rests on her hands
    while her eyes scan her colorful book.

She wears a leopard-print coat
    and mis-matched gloves: one pink,
    one black with grey stripes.

No, that isn't right.
She took her gloves off because she was hot.

Already hot.
Children so warm.
Little furnaces of biology.

She looks up and smiles.
"Was your diabetes like this?"
she asks, points at a page.

No, that isn't right.
She asked me to read the page –
in my head, not aloud.

The pictures show a young woman
(maybe the babysitter)
with signs of wooziness, then
falling asleep into a plate of food.

"It was a lot like that," I tell her.

We came here for hot chocolate
a few years ago and she spilled
her cup all over the floor.

No, that isn't right.
It was our son.

He thought I would be mad.

No that isn't right.
He was mad at himself
because he lost his hot chocolate.

Our daughter's chin rests on her hands
while her eyes scan back and forth
over her colorful book.

She tells me she thinks she needs glasses.
She is seven years old.
She is seven years old and tells me
    the chalkboard at school seems fuzzy.
She tells me that's why she stands
    too close to the television.

We are flawed, she and I.
We are flawed and in need of assistance.
No, that isn't right.

BREAKING THE CYCLE OF REFRIGERATION

I no longer depend on air conditioning,
preferring instead to suffer
inside the sweltering interior
of my 2003 Hyundai, windows rolled up,
sun blasting my chest through the windshield,
so stuffy, impossible to breath
with this sweat-soaked collar around my neck.
I cannot take the cool air against my steaming, pale skin.
I'd rather melt into a puddle of goop,
and spill all over the grey upholstery,
than turn on the cold, forced air,
than let that chill, freonic breeze
make its way over my thin, brittle arms
and shiny, perspiring forehead.
No, I'd rather turn liquid,
turn liquid and drown into myself,
all the while staring straight into that sky-born
ball of gas thinking of some relief besides a/c,
thinking of you.

RED LIGHT GREEN LIGHT

A wind

      like your angry breath

blows across my shorn crown.

I'm reminded

      of how you used to leap from the car

whenever a stoplight interrupted

Just so

      I'd stick my head out the window

and yell for you to get back inside.

COUNTRY LAMENT 252

It's so early in the morning
Where are you? Where are you?
It's so early in the morning
Where are you?

I cannot seem to find you
How that morning sun can blind you
Oh, it's so early in the morning
Where are you?

Seems I woke up just to miss you
Seems I'll never be the same
Seems this heart'll have to make do
That's the one rule of this game

Oh these tossed and turmoiled sheets
And my fuzzy scrambled head
Them satellites circle above me
And this is what they said

It's so early in the morning
Where are you? Where are you?
It's so early in the morning
Where are you?

I cannot seem to find you
How that morning sun can blind you
Oh, it's so early in the morning
Where are you?

My bare feet touch the cold floor
Then I shuffle down the hall
Tired bones they fuss and sputter
This old house with bare, white walls

I step out on the back porch
Pray this day will bring you here
Along with birdsong, new, bright blossoms
And your voice ticklin' my ears

It's so early in the morning
Where are you? Where are you?
It's so early in the morning
Where are you?

I cannot seem to find you
How that morning sun can blind you
Oh, it's so early in the morning
Where are you?

I didn't mean to scare you
Little darling, precious light
Never thought I might upset you
With the words I spoke last night

Now you've gone and up and left me
Sweet lord, what have you left me?
It's so lonely here this morning
Without you

It's so early in the morning
Where are you? Where are you?
It's so early in the morning
Where are you?

I cannot seem to find you
How that morning sun can blind you
Oh, it's so early in the morning
Where are you?

FLORIMELL'S PARALLEL

the rain fell up in ropy lines
    the day he finally left
the sun then froze a crystal blue
    the day he finally left
the insects sang a punk rock tune
    the day he finally left
the oak trees grew metallic spines
    the day he finally left
the day he finally left
    itchy lips kissed sticky pines
the day he finally left
    painted face a purple raccoon
the day he finally left
    tongue slurped sweet, dandelion stew
the day he finally left
    rainropes twisted and entwined

LIFE LONGS FOR ITSELF

Falling snow harmonizes
a child's sense of wonder and the parent in me
wants to stop you running barefoot outside,
hands to heaven, twirling, tongue poised for the sky's gift
in an ancient celebration of being alive.

Political unrest harmonizes
a child's sense of justice and the parent in me
wants to stop you from stumbling blindly into the fray,
slap the slogans from your mouth,
cull from your voice any and all names and opinions
about what is wrong and wicked
with this wandering world.

Yes, the parent in me
wants to stop you right where you are
and say some magic words to stop you
right where you are,
magic words my own parents taught me
but which I counter-spelled with efficiency,

magic words that are worth nothing to any parent ever

except me right here and now

wanting to stop you right where you are,

stop you in time,

just this single time,

stop you in time

to whisper,

"..."

* A RHETORICAL QUESTION IS A FIGURE OF SPEECH IN THE FORM OF A QUESTION THAT IS ASKED IN ORDER TO MAKE A POINT RATHER THAN TO ELICIT AN ANSWER

* see Appendix Q

Who could all this be for if not you?
                          y o u
                            y   o   u

This "I"? This "v"?
This simple, slow rhythm gently galloping along the page?
This golden-beaked finch in my left hand?
This whale in my aching belly?
This trembling lip holding back a sputtering flood?
This supple caress of your tired thigh?
This silent shout across the evening horizon?
This blinding, crippling insight?
Who, if not you?

This quaking desire crumbling to dust every holy temple?
This blistering heat setting fire to every last library?
This loverly confusion occluding every way?
This exasperated existence defined by your name?
Whose name, if not yours?

Whose face to dream, if not yours?
Whose body to enlighten, if not yours?
Whose soul to ignite, if not yours?
Who? Who? Like a goddamn owl, if not you?
Tell me.

Tell me.
Whisper it to me. Sneak into my room.
In the early afternoon. Whisper your name.

THE ANDROGEM PARADOX

Forever my balding head has wanted to write you a poem. But my balding head lives in fear of its own voice, feels limited by its lack of follicles about the crown and forehead.

Today, however, tonight, however, maybe tomorrow, however, my balding head is going to call you on the telephone, however, going to e-mail, however, text, however, Snapchat you a message, a missive, light and airy, fluffy with a bit of under-shine, going to pen you a poem about listening to The Jimi Hendrix Experience the night of May 23rd, 1991, while drinking Strawberry Hill, while drinking Purple Passion, while drinking Milwaukee's Best, while drinking Mickey's, while drinking Southern Comfort, while drinking Everclear, while puking from having drunk so much, every timid follicle nauseated, looking for a truck stop and a cup of coffee, my balding head holding its balding head in its hands as a waitress asks if everything's OK and my balding head finally writes a poem about looking up at this tired creature balancing on a dirty, plastic tray two Diet Dr. Peppers with a pair of extra-long straws and blerbing back at her, "Should this be so tricky?" to which the waitress, God bless her, answers, "I'm not so certain," before walking off to tend to her other, more hirsute tables.

DEPARTURE/CHANGE/SELF/LOSS

The Purple Wizard sighs and smiles and hugs us all
                    with a tight, tender regret.

The Purple Wizard leaves behind 1,000 years
                    of future mystery.

The Purple Wizard sets a brittle, bone alarm clock
                    to "Next Time".

The Purple Wizard enters a deep and cold sea white.

his story is about cool sightings of pigions.I hope you en
joy this amazing story.By! Pill later :'.

We will begin by watching aflock of pigions circleing a tall
,well i guss 2 tall buildings.It looks like a type of dive tha
t looks like a pigion itself andwhile they are going around t
he building they are sooperating.25 minutes later.Now they are
froming back into thatbig bird shape again.It seems like thei
r is a nest at the top of one of the 2 buildings because they
are landingon it.Then they come out of the nest and do their b
ig bird shape again.They also seem to be going behind the buil
ding.But lets hope the first one is true!:_).Thats all i have
got to say so bye and have a good day!:.s. I will be writing
soon again but i think my sister (Her name is Bebe) will be wr
iting a story then it will be my turn to write again!Also i th
ink my next story (mabye article) will be something really coo
l!So stay tuned for the next magzine of The KM Paper.Bebes
next story (/article) might be pretty cool to!So bye4!:0.Have
a very good pleasnt amazing awesome rest of the day!See you
later alligater!:)

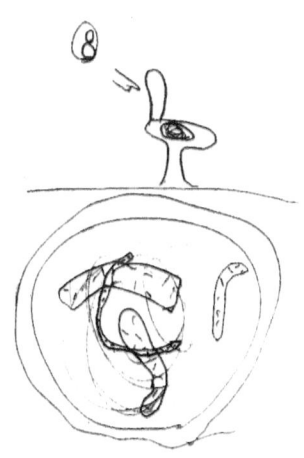

PRAYER OF THE MAGI

A time	before conflict.
An age	without antagonists.
Tigers	hunt flesh.
Birds	rarely rest.

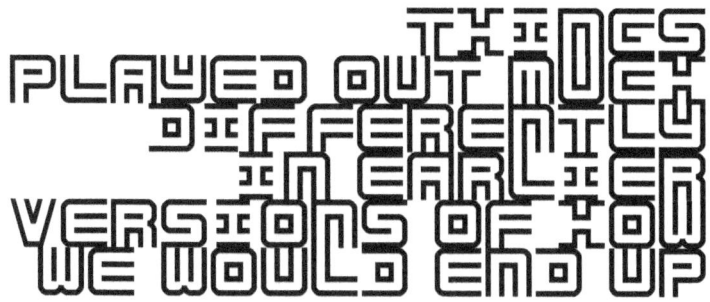

THINGS PLAYED OUT MOSTLY DIFFERENTLY IN EARLIER VERSIONS OF HOW WE WOULD END UP

There would have been toes
lightly gripping the edges of the stairs.
We never locked the doors at night.
We never felt threatened by without.
We imagined music playing: sultry R&B.
Never wanted to close the windows
or even wear a pair of shoes.
We know a load of damp laundry sat
waiting for a roll in the dryer.
The cat roamed where once forbidden.
The dog ate all the trash. The fish floated belly up.
A quiet storm raged and when we showed up
there was nothing silent or slowed.
All was flux. All was how we left it.
Au naturel.

THE ICE CREAM MAN IS COMING

I watched your head roll off your body and down the dark stairwell and through the open door, down the front stoop, through the garden, past the gate, and into the middle of the street where it was promptly squashed by an ice cream truck speeding through our neighborhood.

I watched you chase after your head, stumbling and fumbling.

I watched, from our window, as you held your head's pulpy remains in your lap, chest heaving up and down, unable to cry, unable to wail, but still able to shake an angry fist toward the fading echoes of mulberry bushes.

I SEEM TO RECALL BEING SHOWN A WAY

I have whiled away years doing nothing at all.
I have studied belly-up cockroaches on bathroom floors
and driven past children in diapers meandering the streets.
And I have sat idly by while other men build and buy and
trade and acquire and win and lose. I have breathed ever-
so-slowly as masses of track-suited citizens hustle and
bustle by. I've watched men climb cliffs and dive headfirst
into chilly, dark waters. I sat there on the cliff's edge and
didn't reach out to warn them. Didn't extend a hand,
a thought, any good luck. I've listened to men talk, talk,
talk about the way the world is and who should be
admired and who should be admonished
without responding yay or nay.

All this time I have sat and am sitting still, observing
with intent from afar, mind full of weary wonder.
And I have seen you replace worn shoes
and outdated slacks and stained shirts.
Yes, I have whiled away all these
years waiting, for what I don't know.

YOU CANNOT FIX EVERYTHING FOREVER

The last time you looked, you swore you were alone
Yet now a warm breath bathes the back of your neck
You scour the corners for cracks where the souls seep in
And when you find a fracture you've a putty at the ready –
    a putty made from fish guts and fear
Still the body-less breath remains, so light in form, so –

               Tell us what you see!
               Tell us what you see there!

Tell us how the breath moves from your neck to your
earlobes to your shoulders to your breasts to your naval
how it grows heavy as it draws toward your inner thigh.
The last time you looked, you swore you were alone
Yet now a hot breath captures your every attention
You've all but forgotten the cracks at the corners, souls
squeezing in, putty jar tossed to the floor, rusted blade –
    rusted blade of a putty knife shoved deep down
And that body-less breath breathes everywhere,
so full in execution,

               so –

LIKE LIGHT THIS EXPANDS AND WE NEVER GET WHERE WE ARE GOING

I have an again
and again fantasy
that I can move so fast
that I pass right through you.

Maybe you
felt some grief
some minor discomfort
but mainly your heart
just skipped a beat
forcing you to catch your breath
pause
ask yourself
how I got behind you so quickly
and with such little effort.

ORNITHOLOGY ABANDONS ATHENA

Your scorched throat calls out to nothing,
    nothing but rotten owls.
Owls, for so long so wise, dining on infinity.
Now there is no time left to sustain
    their elevated metabolisms.
They're starving, hunting anything that moves.
Yet you dodge them so professionally,
    have done so all your life,
    let them pass right overhead
    with a wave of your hand
    and an unbroken stride,
    leave them decomposing in the treetops
    ever hungry for just a little more time.

NEXT TIME YOU
ARE FEELING
BLUE JUST LET
A SMILE BEGIN
HAPPY THINGS
WILL COME TO YOU

Just like Smurfs, we scurry for the cover of mushrooms
at the slightest hint of a failed wizard. We are so blue.
None but us seem to understand the danger
of a failed wizard.

Enough misdirected power and cobbled know-how
inflict untold damages.

Lives lustful, greedy –
smell of sweet sewage and sulfur.
Failed wizards try first to lure you
in with nearness and dearness but their wills are not
so steadfast as to forever hold up such a facade.
You tell them, "So sorry, but that was the last MGD,"
and,
"So very sorry, but that really truly was the last MGD."

That's when misspoken magical words, and comes to your
neighborhood an ignorant threat.
That's when the lightning trolls and the flaming rhinos
and the blood blizzards and the mosquito hurricanes.

What can we do but wait it out
in our soft and spongy mushroom homes?
We are so blue, so scared, so teeny-tiny,
prone to gettin' squished.

What can we do every time but wait it out?

We are so blue
and failed wizards are so tall and full of dusty robes
and everyone else only turns the other cheek at their
maniacal laughs and their yellow snaggleteeth.

We are just so blue.

Only so blue.

THE AFTERPARTY

♥♫♥♫♥♫♥♫♥♫♥♫♥♫

The sound of your voice like corn stalks
swimming together in a pool of midnight ...
Remember the time we left The Outhouse,
after the Alice Donut show,
moonshined bodies, 1 in the morning,

And we tumbled into the corn fields
thinking we'd run through them,
And it would be like a movie,
plants falling before our lovers' dream,
Bowing in polite deference
to human whimsy and romance?

But instead, those proud, tall bastards showed
a will of their own, a vengeance, a desire to tell us
to shut the fuck up and go home already,

Yet without mouths and voiceboxes and lungs
all they could do was ...

All they could do was ...

All they could do was clog our noses
and noiseholes with tightly-woven tassels,

All they could do was choke us to sleep
with sweet shimmery cornsilk.
And remember how we slept there in the cornfields,
sweetly cocooned, purple-faced and starved for oxygen?
Remember how we pulled blood-covered stamens
from each other's mouths with such desperate, tender love?
Remember spewing plant matter onto the dry ground
and swearing that the dried corn leaves underfoot spelled out:

"Reconsider"?

God,
my dear,
those were the days, our days,
so young and wild and free.

NEVER TRUST A HEAVENLY BODY

Oh! How I love to watch the night sky
suckle
from the milking moon overhead!

The moon that's waited for years
for a black-holed transformation
but somehow wound up sharing space
with ice-covered rings of dust.

A vast
and light-filled vacuum
promised that moon
the world,
the World!

FUTURE DEATHS LEAVE A STAINED PAST FROM WHENCE ARE BORN CHILDREN OF NIGHT

Come, let us flee
from the coming dawn.
Let us lock every door,
pull the shades down low.
    Let us live like vampires,
    like ancient predators.
    Let us hide from the world,
    until ready to feast on it.
Pull me over you, soldier on,
carry on, war metaphors
hang between us, red in the air,
arousing our blood senses.
    So we hearken to darkness,
    to pre-civil structures
    that lurk, as we do,
    deep in black murk shadows.

MUTTERING TO ONESELF CURIOUS

When next you are alone
drop to your hands and knees.
Crawl to the northwest corner
of wherever you may be.

When you reach that corner
take your finger long and straight,
push it through the corner
until a tiny hole you make.

When you feel that hole appear
remove your fingertip.
Bend close to take a peek now
at what moves behind the rip.

The monsters that you see there
are fed by countless frights.
So when you poke dark corners
keep your breathing slow and tight.

US V. THEM

We are hurricanes
They are wildfires

We are plagues of locusts
They are storms of frogs

We are Anthrax
They are Ebola

We are tumors caused by cell phones
They are imbalanced microbiomes

We are fingers slammed in a car door
They are tongues burnt by hot soup

We are teeth scraping cold concrete
They are heads slamming through a windshield

We are every unanswered prayer
They are every campaign promise

Yes, we are steady earthquakes
And they, they are patient volcanoes

HEARING IS
SEEING IS
BELIEVING

I hear
"like the blind
leading the blind"

with the
implication
being they'll fall

into a pit
or off a cliff
but it's been

my experience
that folks without sight
are way more cautious

than all that.

Absence Metabolic Makes The Heart Grow Fonder

As a youth
he'd pluck the wings
from butterflies ...

Some misguided
perverse attempt
to reverse metamorphosis ...

Didn't comprehend
in the green then
being built of fevered dreams ...

The sun
rising
in the west ...

The earth
dead center
of the cosmos ...

AS FALLS

I woke to a dream dissolving:
You, buried under the Flint Hills,
at the bottom of a grassy green sea,
where once a blue sea,
leviathans,
now you, with a pen in hand.
And underneath the Flint Hills,
you wrote your own epitaph.
On a dinosaur bone,
you wrote, "Here lies one
with words and time,"
and you cinched it
to a grey balloon
then you sent it up with a kiss
to announce your final resting place
after another million years of erosion.
I dreamed the Flint Hills
as a named subdivision
in a shining, Wichita suburb,
every cozy house a tombstone
over a hundred long-buried yous.

The Silence Over Oppression by Otherwise Good People

Awash in remembered sounds,
alone and clinging
to a cold, bald mountaintop.

So many tricks the brain plays to entertain itself,
    to distract itself,
    to soothe itself,
    to forget itself.

Over and over the sights and sounds
and over and over and over the thoughts and the tragedies,
    and the thoughts of thoughts of the tragedies,

        and the thoughts of the thoughts of the thoughts.

Alone on a mountain silent,
unforgiving melodies
plague our brains
until the sun quiets down.

ONCE BROKEN THEN OPEN

Narrative robs our breath
when we watch
to remember.

We have religion
because we die.
So let us hope
we suffer well.

Vulnerability is a gift
and our tears
fall like confetti.

●
●
●
●

THE OLDER ONE RECOGNIZES REGRETS AND ATTEMPTS TO RECTIFY THE SITUATION

Underneath

that old sink

you will find

your lost wings.

Put them on.

Fly away.

I was wrong

to hide them.

Forgive me.

Do not wait.

Soon you will

become a

miracle.

WE FEAR WE HAVE FRIGHTED

I hear the horns of our doom in the distance and

I hear Spanish cries of love and anguish and heartache only I've forgotten all the Spanish I used to know but I can feel these are the subjects of their wailing, echoing voices and

I hear a washboard rubbed up and down like a saucy lover on a sweaty, summer day and I hear the luscious lisps of Latina luchadoras leaping from the top rope into the arms of lucky lovers
and

I hear a cowbell and need more, always and

I hear you whispering in the quiet spaces, where the horns of our doom take siesta, where the horns of doom turn away from the prior horrors they've wrought, where the horns of our doom pretend the future isn't brass at all, but

a glowing,
rhythmic
holy
pulse of silicon and fiber optics and
now

I listen for the sound of light moving through glass but only hear something that sounds like nothing and nothing is not what my ears long for at this moment,

no,
certainly not with those brash and ballsy
horns of doom marching our way ...

ROYAL AND WRINKLED WITH AGE

On a scrap of paper,
blown by the wind
across my feet,
I found these words
in coal dust writ:

"The Purple Wizard stands on a barren hillside
facing the rising sun.
The Purple Wizard's greywhite hair circles 'round
and 'tween proud, bony legs.
In the left hand, the Purple Wizard holds a crooked staff
carved from mastodon bone.
The right hand holds
a dense ball of red-brown fire ants,
swarming and angry.

The Purple Wizard expects to live forever and knows
the name of every star from here to when.
The Purple Wizard never was a child and never lost

anything,
neither legs nor lunch.

The Purple Wizard knows the secrets of the waterwood
true and the Purple Wizard inhales ash,
swims through death like
a swordfish, cunning and complete.

Many loves and hates had the Purple Wizard
and many minds did unfurl.
When the rains came
and the flowers finally bloomed,
only the Purple Wizard felt morose,
only the Purple Wizard felt
      responsible,
only the Purple Wizard remained on a barren
      hill to apologize."

> I let the winds
> scoop the paper
> then turn my face
> toward the North

> continue down the path.

Once there was a soldier who needed to get home. His name was Tod and his sister had been kidnaped by Distructer of the Butter. While he was trying to travel home he saw a troll who was green and ugly. The troll looked nice, but what the soldier didn't know was that the troll was one of Distructer of the Butter's spy. The soldier made friends with the troll and the troll decided to not work for DB anymore. The soldier told the troll about Jinavi who loved him but also how he didn't love her. A day later, they stubled across a sly dragon. He was red and green. He started to fight them for no reason, and so they ran away.

Task 1: crossing the crocidile river. The two of them had t

APPENDIX @
SPONTANEOUS COMBUSTION/ENLIGHTENMENT

www.ingramcontent.com/pod-product-compliance
Lightning Source LLC
Chambersburg PA
CBHW020624300426
44113CB00007B/770